Riddl...
tongue-tu...
also found...
our pages. Do you know where's
the peck of pickled peppers
Peter Piper picked?
Have you any idea how many
pop-bottles Pop bottles?
Meet the first bionic boy who would love
to have a bionic brain . . .
and sister Jane who is nothing
but a big black crow . . .
and the Ning Nang Nong
where the cows go bong . . . and the
man who sells monkey business.
How absurd!
We hope so. We hope, too, you will
have as much fun reading these
comic poems as we have had
collecting them.

Zenka and Ian Woodward

Contents

First edition

© LADYBIRD BOOKS LTD MCMLXXXIII

COMIC AND CURIOUS VERSE

chosen by Zenka and Ian Woodward
illustrated by Pat Oakley of Hurlston Design

Ladybird Books Loughborough

Intelligence test

'What do you use your eyes for?'
The white-coated man enquired.
'I use my eyes for looking,'
Said Toby, ' – unless I'm tired.'

'I see. And then you close them,'
Observed the white-coated man.
'Well done. A very good answer.
Let's try another one.'

'What is your nose designed for?
What use is the thing to you?'
'I use my nose for smelling,'
Said Toby. 'Don't you, too?'

'I do indeed,' said the expert,
'That's what the thing is for.
Now I've another question to ask you,
Then there won't be any more.'

'What are your ears intended for?
Those things at each side of your head?
Come on — don't be shy — I'm sure you can say.'
'For washing behind,' Toby said.

Vernon Scannell

The bionic boy

It really fills me full of joy
To be the first bionic boy;
To know that I have got the power
To run at sixty miles an hour,

To punch my way through doors and walls,
To juggle with three cannon-balls,
To rope a steer or buffalo,
To tie a steel rod in a bow,

To uproot trees, break out of jails,
To fight successfully with whales,
To stop the traffic in the Strand
By waving my bionic hand,
To swim to Cap Gris-Nez and back
And then lay low the whole Welsh pack.

There's just one thing I must explain,
I haven't a bionic brain;
A matter of profound regret,
For I've no 'O'-levels as yet.

Charles Connell

Father says

Father says
Never
let
me
see
you
doing
that
again
Father says
tell you once
tell you a thousand times
come hell or high water
his finger drills my shoulder
never let me see you doing that again

My brother knows all his phrases off by heart
so we practise them in bed at night.

Michael Rosen

You were the mother last time

'You were the mother last time.
It's my turn today.'
        'It's *my* turn.'
'No, *my* turn.'
        'All right then, I won't play.'
'Oh, go ahead then, *be* the mother.
It's not fair
But I don't care.'

'I was the father last time.
I won't be today.'
        'It's your turn.'
'No, *your* turn.'
        'All right then, I won't play.'
'Oh, never mind, *don't* be the father.
It's not fair
But I don't care.'

'I was the sister last time.
It's your turn today.'
  'It is not.'
'It is so.'
  'All right then, I won't play.'
'Oh, never mind, *don't* be the sister.
It's not fair
But I don't care.'

'I have an idea!
Let's *both* be mothers!
(We'll pretend
About the others.)'

Mary Ann Hoberman

My sister Jane

And I say nothing — no, not a word
About our Jane. Haven't you heard
She's a bird, a bird, a bird, a bird.
Oh it never would do to let folks know
My sister's nothing but a great big crow.

Each day (we daren't send her to school)
She pulls on stockings of thick blue wool
To make her pin crow legs look right,
Then fits a wig of curls on tight,
And dark spectacles — a huge pair
To cover her very crowy stare.
Oh it never would do to let folks know
My sister's nothing but a great big crow.

When visitors come she sits upright
(With her wings and her tail tucked out of sight).
They think her queer but extremely polite.
Then when the visitors have gone
She whips out her wings and with her wig on
Whirls through the house at the height of your head —
Duck, duck, or she'll knock you dead.
Oh it never would do to let folks know
My sister's nothing but a great big crow.

At meals whatever she sees she'll stab it —
Because she's a crow and that's a crow habit.
My mother says, 'Jane! Your manners! Please!'
Then she'll sit quietly on the cheese,
Or play the piano nicely by dancing on the keys —
Oh it never would do to let folks know
My sister's nothing but a great big crow.

Ted Hughes

14

Bucket

Every evening after tea
grandad would take his bucket for a walk

An empty bucket

When I asked him why
he said because it was easier to carry
than a full one

grandad had
an answer
for everything

Roger McGough

Dougal MacDougal

A bugler named Dougal MacDougal
Found ingenious ways to be frugal.
He learned how to sneeze
In various keys,
Thus saving the price of a bugle.

Ogden Nash

What they do

Cocks crow,
Hens lay.
Cocks know
Break-o'-day,
Hens tell
Break-o'-shell.
Cocks crow,
Hens lay.

Eleanor Farjeon

A thought

If I were John and John were Me,
Then he'd be six and I'd be three.
If John were Me and I were John,
I shouldn't have these trousers on.

A A Milne

Peter Piper

Peter Piper picked a peck of pickled peppers;
A peck of pickled peppers Peter Piper picked.
If Peter Piper picked a peck of pickled peppers,
Where's the peck of pickled peppers Peter Piper
picked?

Unknown

Well, I never!

A doctor fell in a deep well
    And broke his collar bone.
The Moral: Doctor, mind the sick
    And leave the well alone.

Unknown

On the Ning Nang Nong

On the Ning Nang Nong
Where the Cows go Bong!
And the Monkeys all say Boo!
There's a Nong Nang Ning
Where the trees go Ping!
And the tea pots Jibber Jabber Joo.
On the Nong Ning Nang
All the mice go Clang!
And you just can't catch 'em when they do!

So it's Ning Nang Nong!
Cows go Bong!
Nong Nang Ning!
Trees go Ping!
Nong Ning Nang!
The mice go Clang!
What a noisy place to belong,
Is the Ning Nang Ning Nang Nong!

Spike Milligan

21

Song of the pop-bottlers

Pop bottles pop-bottles
    In pop shops;
The pop-bottles Pop bottles
    Poor Pop drops.

When Pop drops pop-bottles
    Pop-bottles plop!
Pop-bottle-tops topple!
    Pop mops slop!

Stop! Pop'll drop bottle!
    Stop, Pop, stop!
When Pop bottles pop-bottles,
    Pop-bottles pop!

Morris Bishop

Toodley Gronickpet:
The goblin bagpiper

Puff Puff Puff Puff
Into the bag I blow,
Puff Puff Puff Puff,
Ying Tong Iddle I Po.
Puff Puff Puff Puff
I try to fill it with air.

If I don't pump it up
With a hip! and a hup!
I can't get a tune out of there!
So, Puff Puff Puff Puff
Oh what's the use of trying
Whatever tune I try to play
It sounds as if I'm dying.

Spike Milligan

Skateboarder

I can soar, I can swoop,
I can buckle at will,
I've tried looping the loop,
I've touched fifty downhill.

I've done end-over-end, I've shot into the sky,
I zoom down, then ascend,
Gravity I defy.

I am flirting with death
As I hang there in space,
I am holding my breath
For I'm winning this race.

I am moving so fast
That my vision is blurred.
I am flying at last —
I'm a bird! I'm a bird!

Charles Connell

Sir Smasham Uppe

Good afternoon, Sir Smasham Uppe!
We're having tea: do take a cup!
Sugar and milk? Now let me see —
Two lumps, I think? . . . Good gracious me!
The silly thing slipped off your knee!
Pray don't apologise, old chap:
A very trivial mishap!
So clumsy of you? How absurd!
My dear Sir Smasham, not a word!

Now do sit down and have another,
And tell us all about your brother —
You know, the one who broke his head.
Is the poor fellow still in bed?
A chair — allow me, sir! . . . Great Scott!
That *was* a nasty smash! Eh, what?
Oh, not at all: the chair was old —
Queen Anne, or so we have been told.
We've got at least a dozen more:
Just leave the pieces on the floor.

I want you to admire our view:
Come nearer to the window, do;
And look how beautiful . . . Tut, tut!
You didn't see that it was shut?
I hope you are not badly cut!
Not hurt? A fortunate escape!
Amazing! Not a single scrape!
And now, if you have finished tea,
I fancy you might like to see
A little thing or two I've got.

That china plate? Yes, worth a lot:
A beauty too . . . Ah, there it goes!
I trust it didn't hurt your toes?
Your elbow brushed it off the shelf?
Of course: I've done the same myself.
And now, my dear Sir Smasham — Oh,
You surely don't intend to go?
You *must* be off? Well, come again,
So glad you're fond of porcelain.

E V Rieu

You tell me

Here are the football results:
League Division Fun
Manchester United won, Manchester City lost.
Crystal Palace 2, Buckingham Palace 1
Millwall Leeds nowhere
Wolves 8 A cheese roll and had a cup of tea 2
Aldershot 3 Buffalo Bill shot 2
Evertonill, Liverpool's not very well either
Newcastle's Heaven Sunderland's a very nice place 2
Ipswich one? You tell me.

Michael Rosen

Business

Don Arturo says:
There was a man
who sold puppets and whistles
for a living
He also played guitar
he used to go
to the shopping areas
and draw huge crowds
They bought his whistles
and puppets
They threw money into
his guitar
This was against the law
So he was arrested at
least three times a week

When his turn came up
in the courtroom
He took a puppet out
and put a show on
All the detectives
and court clerks
rolled on the floor
When he finished
they all bought puppets
and whistles from him
The judge got angry
and yelled:
What kind of business
is this
And the man said
I am the monkey man
and the
monkey man sells
monkey business.

Victor Hernández Cruz

34

Down the stream the swans all glide

Down the stream the swans all glide;
It's quite the cheapest way to ride.
Their legs get wet,
Their tummies wetter:
I think after all
The bus is better.

Spike Milligan

Eletelephony

Once there was an elephant,
Who tried to use the telephant —
No! No! I mean an elephone
Who tried to use the telephone —
(Dear me! I am not certain quite
That even now I've got it right.)

Howe'er it was, he got his trunk
Entangled in the telephunk;
The more he tried to get it free,
The louder buzzed the telephee —
(I fear I'd better drop the song
Of elephop and telephong!)

Laura E Richards

The lion

Oh, weep for Mr and Mrs Bryan!
He was eaten by a lion;
Following which, the lion's lioness
Up and swallowed Bryan's Bryaness.

Ogden Nash

Can a parrot

Can a parrot
Eat a carrot
Standing on his head?
If I did that my mum would send me
Straight upstairs to bed.

Spike Milligan

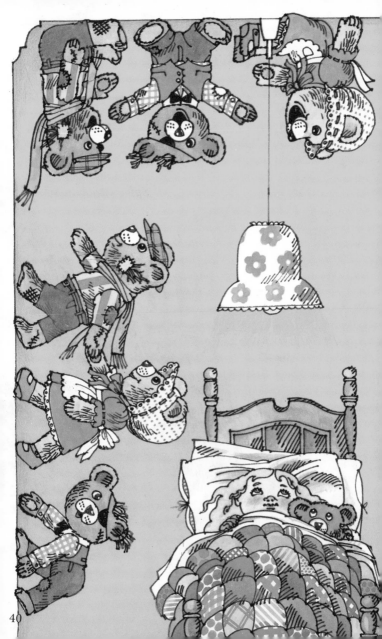

Night-bears

Three little bears
From nowhere in particular,
    nowhere in particular,
    nowhere at all,
Came up the stairs
And climbed the perpendicular,
    climbed the perpendicular,
    nursery wall.

They sat upon the ceiling
And sang with all their might
Songs so full of feeling
They lasted half the night.

A funny thing it seemed
For little bears to do.
I think I must have dreamed
Those little bears, don't you?

For when the songs were ended
Then down the wall they slid,
And when they had descended
Do you know what they did?

Those three little bears
Went nowhere in particular,
    nowhere in particular,
    flat or perpendicular,
    nowhere at all.

Wilma Horsbrugh

Who's in

'The door is shut fast
And everyone's out.'
But people don't know
What they're talking about!
Says the fly on the wall,
And the flame on the coals,

And the dog on his rug,
And the mice in their holes,
And the kitten curled up,
And the spiders that spin —
'What, everyone's out?
Why, everyone's in!'

Elizabeth Fleming

43

821.008 Com

Acknowledgments

*Permission to reprint copyright material
has been granted as follows:*

"Song of the pop-bottlers" by Morris Bishop from
A Bowl of Bishop by permission of The Dial Press;
"The bionic boy" and "Skateboarder" by Charles Connell, from
Versicles and Limericks, by permission of the Hamlyn Publishing
Group Ltd; "Business" by Victor Hernandez Cruz, from Mainland,
copyright 1973 Victor Hernandez Cruz, by permission of Random House
Inc; "What they do" by Eleanor Farjeon, from The Children's Bells (Oxford
University Press) by permission of David Higham Associates as the author's
agents; "Who's in" by Elizabeth Fleming from In Poem Town by permission
of Alison Fleming; "You were the mother last time" by Mary Ann Hoberman,
from Not Enough Bed for the Babies by permission of Russell and Volkening
as agents for the author; "Night bears" from The Bold Bad Bus by Wilma
Horsbrugh by permission of the author; "My sister Jane" by Ted Hughes from
Meet My Folks (copyright 1961, 1973) by permission of The Bobbs-Merrill
Company Inc and Faber and Faber Ltd; "Bucket" by Roger McGough (copyright
1976 by Roger McGough) from You Tell Me by permission of Tessa Sayle as agent
for the author; "Can a parrot", "Down the stream the swans all glide", and "On
the Ning Nang Nong" by Spike Milligan from Silly Verse for Kids by permission
of Norma Farnes as author's agent; "Toodley Gronickpet: The Goblin Bagpiper"
from Goblins by Spike Milligan by permission of the Hutchinson Publishing
Group, and Norma Farnes as author's agent; "A thought" by A A Milne
from Now We Are Six (copyright 1927 by EP Dutton and Co Inc, renewed
1955 by A A Milne) by permission of the publisher, EP Dutton Inc, Associated
Book Publishers Ltd, and the Canadian publishers, McClelland and
Stewart Ltd; "Dougal MacDougal" (copyright 1940, Ogden Nash) and
"The lion" (copyright 1944, Ogden Nash) from Verses from 1929 On
(copyright 1944, 1959 by Ogden Nash) by permission of Curtis Brown
Ltd, and Little, Brown and Company; "Eletelephony" by Laura
E Richards from Tirra Lirra: Rhymes Old and New (copyright 1932
by Laura E Richards, renewed 1960 by Hamilton Richards) by
permission of Little, Brown and Company; "Sir Smasham
Uppe" by E V Rieu by permission of Miss Penelope Rieu;
"Father says" by Michael Rosen from Mind Your Own
Business (1974 edition) appears by permission of Andre
Deutsch Ltd; "You tell me" by Michael Rosen from
You Tell Me (Puffin Books 1981) by permission
of Penguin Books Ltd; "Intelligence test" by
Vernon Scannell, from The Apple
Raid, appears by permission
of the author